GARETH FARR

Gareth Farr has been an actor for over twelve years working at the RSC, Young Vic, West End, Royal Court, West Yorkshire Playhouse and Sheffield Theatres, as well as numerous television roles on programmes including *Misfits*, *Skins* and *Vera*. He is now the Head of Acting at Arts Educational Schools London. He has always been a writer and was part of the Royal Court's new-writing scheme and Super-Group. *Britannia Waves the Rules* won a Judges Award at the 2011 Bruntwood Prize for Playwriting and is his first full-length, professionally produced play.

Other Titles in this Series

Gareth Farr

BRITANNIA WAVES THE RULES

NICK HERN BOOKS

London

www.nickhernbooks.co.uk

A Nick Hern Book

Britannia Waves the Rules first published in Great Britain as a paperback original in 2014 by Nick Hern Books Limited, The Glasshouse, 49a Goldhawk Road, London W12 8QP

Cover image: photo by Simon Pantling, illustration by Daren Newman, Me & My Pen

Designed and typeset by Nick Hern Books, London
Printed in Great Britain by Mimeo Ltd, Cambridgeshire PE29 6XX

A CIP catalogue record for this book is available from the British Library

ISBN 978 1 84842 386 2

Britannia Waves the Rules was first performed at the Royal Exchange Theatre, Manchester, on 27 May 2014, with the following cast:

CARL'S MUM	Clare Calbraith
BILKO/ANDY APPLETON/ ENSEMBLE	Simon Harrison
CARL JACKSON	Dan Parr
CARL'S DAD/UNCLE CHARLES/ANTHONY APPLETON/ENSEMBLE	Colin Tierney
GOLDIE SHAW/ENSEMBLE	Francesca Zoutewelle

Director	Nick Bagnall
Designer	Ashley Martin-Davis
Lighting Designer	Chris Davey
Sound Designer	Peter Rice
Composer	Alex Baranowski
Movement and Fight Director	Kevin McCurdy
Assistant Director	Liz Stevenson
Casting Director	Jerry Knight-Smith CDG

To Gabby.
For your dignity. For your strength.
For teaching me so much. For holding on and believing.
You are my world.

Acknowledgements

Special thanks to the Bruntwood Prize for Playwriting, the Peggy Ramsay Foundation, Suzanne Bell, Sarah Frankcom, Jamie Samuel, Josh Hayes, Gary Cooper, Katherine Rose Morely and Keeley Forsyth for the development work.

Thanks to John Kettle for the use of his song and lyrics. Thanks to the staff and students of Arts Educational Schools London for their time, patience and support in allowing me to work on this production.

Thanks to Nick Bagnall for his unending passion towards this play. Thanks to my mum and dad for everything. Thanks to Gabby for her patience, support and love.

This play would be so much less without you all.

G.F.

'I know this government bids us choose,
I know a nation stands in queues,
Have you ever been in Room 101? Where the waiting's
    never done.
And I laugh and I cry. Britannia waives the rules.'

'Pendle Hill', The Tansads

Characters

CARL
UNCLE CHARLES
ANDY APPLETON
ANTHONY APPLETON
GOLDIE SHAW
DAD
RECRUITING OFFICER
SERGEANT STOKES
BILKO
CORPORAL
MUM
AFGHAN MAN
LIEUTENANT THOMPSON

This text went to press before the end of rehearsals and so may differ slightly from the play as performed.

Alone on stage CARL *is running. It's graceful and strong and fluid. We watch him. He stops, catches his breath, looks at the audience and recites a poem.*

CARL.
>Nowhere to go and nothing to do,
>Nothing to earn and housekeeping too,
>In a coastal town with a postal frown,
>Because nobody wants to go there.
>
>Everyone knows you and nobody knows you,
>Some people like you but most people hate you,
>They were born here, they still live here.
>Just. Like. You.
>
>'Will you work? Why won't you work?
>Got to get a job and behave.'
>But a job is a wage and a wage is a cage,
>In a town. Like. Mine.
>
>So I reckon I'll wait, I'll bide my time till something
>   better comes along,
>I'm only young; the bottom-est rung.
>So I'll think and I'll sink.
>I'll wander and ponder,
>Till I know. What's. What.
>
>Or maybe I'll just go, and break all the rules of this
>   Alcatraz town,
>Maybe I'll go and not turn back,
>Cos if nowt comes from nowt and owt comes from out,
>I'm better. Off. Gone.

It's a poem. I wrote it. It's shit. I know it's shit.

Have you ever been to Blackpool? Don't bother it's shit. I'm serious. It is, it's shit.

I looked up the word façade once in the dictionary. My Uncle Charles said it so I looked it up. He's fat my Uncle

Charles. He's fat but he doesn't think he is. He thinks he's fit but he's not. He's fat. Fat like with two bellies, where his belt digs into his gut. And he's bald. And he wears glasses. That's about it. He used to take me to the British Legion every Saturday afternoon when I was a kid. I say every Saturday afternoon, he did it for about a year, two years, about eighteen months after his sister died to give my dad a break. His sister, my dad's wife, my mum, she died and he took me to the Legion on Saturdays to give my old man some space. Fuckin' British Legion. Have you ever been in one of those places? Don't bother they're shit. At least the one in Blackpool is.

Somewhere else in the space UNCLE CHARLES *sits by the window of the British Legion.*

The British Legion in dirty old Blackpool town. It was old. Picture of the Queen behind the bar and old. Everything was old. It looked old, it smelled old, it was full of oldness and it was always hot. They used to keep the heating on full so that all the old dudes didn't die. We'd go in and we'd throw our coats in the corner, there were no pegs, just a corner of the room where everyone threw their coats and gloves and stuff in a big pile. Uncle Charles would drop his coat, walk straight over to the bar and order a whiskey and pint of bitter. Knobhead Uncle Charles, proper Blackpool. He'd get his drink then he'd order a Coke or a lemonade or a shandy for me and he'd leave me there waiting for it while he went and sat in his spot. Massive windows they had in there. Like, big yawning windows on one wall, old, single-glazed and clean. They'd be steamed up because of the heating and the damp from the coats and old men and breath. He'd always sit in the same spot and he'd turn his body against the room, his fat gut stretching his shirt, straining the cotton on his buttons and he'd just look out of the steamed-up window. He'd look out of the steamed-up window at the street that we'd just walked down. Always just gazing out of a steamed-up window. I'd play snooker on my own. They're bigger than you think, proper snooker tables.

UNCLE CHARLES. It's just a façade. Blackpool. Nothing more than that. A façade.

CARL. He just said it to no one. I didn't know what he meant so I put down the snooker cue and sat on the floor.

Have you ever been to Blackpool? Don't go it's full of people like my Uncle Charles. He is Blackpool, Uncle Charles. He is Blackpool,

> Quiet, grey, cold and old. Cigarette stains and fool's gold on his fingers.

He's got Blackpool printed in his bones like the rock. He was right though, about the façade. I looked it up in the dictionary. It's a good word. It's got two meanings, the front of a building is one, but what Uncle Charles was driving at was that Blackpool has got a deceptive outward appearance.

Damn right Uncle Charles. It's a trampy, scaggy, shit-stinking toilet but people still turn up here because it's got flashing lights and candyfloss. They get told it's good don't they? It's not good. It's filth and it's full of bastards. It's full of bastards who've been trained to chase other people's money. It's true. They've taught themselves to not feel bad about taking poor people's last coins from their empty pockets and to give them absolutely nothing at all in return. People with money don't come to Blackpool, people without money come to Blackpool and the people from Blackpool are all kicking and biting and scratching and scamming to try and get what they haven't got off them.

That's the façade.

It's bad.

Proper bad.

Not good.

UNCLE CHARLES *finishes his pint, stands up, picks his coat from the floor and leaves. The British Legion scene dissolves into the darkness.*

Uncle Charles. Proper Blackpool that bloke. Written in his bones. His marrow.

Quick shift into a new day. There is an uncomfortable, charged and erratic energy to CARL *now.*

I've had a bad day. It started in the Job Centre and it carried
on. It lasted, it carried on inside me. I'd gone down to the
Job Centre and I'd bumped into the Appletons.

*Somewhere in the space the Job Centre forms. Paper on the
floor, the hum of emptiness.*

It stinks of men who don't wash in the Job Centre. Men who
have no reason to wash. Is there anything more desperate
than that? Dirty breath and eyes with that horrid, crystallised
green shit that you get while you're asleep. I'm not one of
these people and I won't be – but I am because I'm here and
I'm part of the smell. I can't think like that though or I'll get
into a fuckin' rage. There's no Blackpool written on my
bones. No way, no never. I don't want a job because a job is
a wage and a wage is a cage in a town. Like. Mine.

The APPLETONS *enter.*

ANDY. Alright Carl?

CARL (*still with the audience*). And there it is. I knew it was
coming. It had to because it smells of something else in here.
It smells of Blackpool's future, of its present, it smells of the
one thing that does bring in a profit round here, all year
round here, there's money and a market and this boy sells it.

ANTHONY. Alright Carl?

CARL. And so does his brother. The Appletons, two of them,
Anthony and Andy. The Appletons were one of those
families that called their children names that all began with
the same letter, like a code, like a medal, like a patrol.
Andrea was my age and Alan was older and there was
Anthony and Andy, who were twins. They were twins and
they sold drugs and for some reason they liked me.

ANDY. Alright Carl?

CARL. Alright Andy? How's it going?

ANDY. Knockout our kid, knockout.

CARL (*to the audience*). I don't need to tell you who they think
they are do I? They walk with a swagger and they wore
Adidas three-stripes and sunglasses and those stupid fuckin'

sun hats down over their eyes. I don't need to tell you who they think they are do I?

Fuckin' mock-Mancs.

ANTHONY. What you up to?

CARL. Nothing. Just looking, just window-shopping.

ANTHONY. Window-shopping. Window-shopping. You're funny you are Carl.

ANDY. Yeah you should be on that pier mate. Yeah.

CARL. Yeah?

ANDY. Yeah. Sound. Our kid.

CARL. You window-shopping or are you after something special?

ANDY. Oh yeah, something special. Something very special but we're not after it, we've got it.

CARL. Right.

ANTHONY. Best business in here. It's a regular stop on the rounds this place mate. Fuckin' dream factory this place. Everyone's trying to forget summat – make 'emselves feel better, you know how it is.

Do you want some?

CARL. Er no ta mate.

ANDY. Why not?

CARL. It's a bit early for me mate.

ANTHONY. Never too early our kid, not if you don't sleep.

CARL. Not for me.

ANDY. How old are you Carl?

CARL. Why?

ANDY. Because, I'm not kidding, you will be dead in sixty years. Dead and gone and you're not coming back boy. Sixty years – absolute maximum. Less if you stay round here.

Fact. So get on it, get on it hard and enjoy it while you've got it our kid.

ANTHONY. Come on, we'll go for a drive and have a day. Come on Carl, our Andrea is always on about you. She reckons you're a sound bloke. Prove her right, nobody else ever does.

There is anger building within CARL.

CARL. I'm just here to get the paperwork done boys. Sorry.

ANTHONY. Your loss sunshine.

The Job Centre dissolves into darkness. CARL *moves to be with the audience. He is moving, he is active and volatile and charged with something.*

CARL. Pricks. Fuckin' mock-Manc pricks, chatting to me like I need them. I can feel it coming on, something they said, and I don't know what it was but something they said made me click and I can feel it coming on. I'm trying to fight it but I can't, I don't want to, why should I? It's just a rage, I know what to do. I'm on top of them these days. So I'm home, upstairs, into my gear, slam the door, I'm out and away.

CARL *is running. Steady to begin with but getting harder and harder.*

Feeling it hard, like it's gonna be with me all day, like it's on me and in me and steering me and breathing for me and pulsing me and making me clench really bastard hard. It's a rage, just a rage. Straight down the road and onto the seafront. Two miles to the first pier, three miles to the second. Second pier, three miles there, three miles back, six miles to run through the rage. Pissing it down now like one of those days that can't make anything feel good. You could win the Lottery on a day like this, a double rollover, a triple Euromillions rollover with a free cherry-on-top cake and still feel shit. Still. Feel. Really. Shit. And. Nasty. And. Angry. Like it needs to hurt. So I run. I run hard. Till I hurt hard. That's what I do. I need to feel something bad and hard and nasty to take the rage away. Blackpool, look at the state of it. It's shit. It is shit. It's shit that's surrounded by shit. It's floating in the sea and still people kiss its arse.

Lungs. Lungs. Come on. Stitch.

CARL *is running harder.*

Bad-as-fuck Blackpool.

Thigh. Stitch. Faster.

It's a rape victim. People from other places come here and rape it and leave nothing behind. They should send criminals here and make them watch what happens when everything closes up and the lights are turned off and it pisses it down and people cry with rain on their faces on the way to the Job Centre. Stitch. Thigh. Knee. A job is a wage and a wage is a cage. A job is a wage and a wage is a cage in a town. Like. Mine.

Knee. Lungs. Harder. More.

CARL *is running harder.*

> Nowhere to go and nothing to do,
> Nothing to earn and housekeeping too,
> In a coastal town with a postal frown,
> Because nobody wants to go there.

Stitch.

Knee.

> Is a wage and a wage –

Stitch, more, more.

> A wage is a cage. A job is a wage and a wage is a cage.
>   A job is a wage and a wage is a cage.

GOLDIE SHAW *appears somewhere in the space.* CARL *doesn't see her. He is running increasingly harder to get more hurt. She is stood, huddled, sheltering herself from the rain.*

GOLDIE. Carl.

CARL. Knee. Lungs burning, faster, harder.

GOLDIE. Carl.

CARL. First pier. Keep going. Harder faster, more hurt, hamstrings, thighs, chest, chest, chest.

GOLDIE. Carl.

CARL. My name.

GOLDIE. Carl.

CARL. Goldie Shaw is standing in front of me. Right in front of me... all...

He breaks away and talks to the audience.

Goldie Shaw. Fucking Goldie Shaw, you love her already don't you? I mean just look at her. Goldie Shaw. What kind of parents call their daughter Goldie? Confident ones. Confident ones that knew she'd turn out just like she did. Beautiful. Eighteen-carat-solid, fit-as-fuck, Goldie. Her confident, beautiful parents owned the toy shop in Blackpool. There's loads of toy shops in Blackpool but they owned the toy shop that kids from Blackpool went to. Not a tourist toy shop, our toy shop. They had it right. I'd known her since we were at primary school and even then she was set apart. Nine-carat then but she still had it. She had what all the other girls wanted and what all the boys wanted to get hold of.

Goldie. Goldie fuckin' Shaw.

GOLDIE. What were you shouting?

CARL. What?

GOLDIE. You were shouting when you were running. What was it?

CARL. I wasn't shouting. What are you doing here?

GOLDIE. I like it down here. I've seen you before. You run down here quite a lot don't you?

CARL. I've never seen you.

GOLDIE. I've never called out before.

CARL. Right.

CARL speaks to the audience.

Silence, there's a silence, not a real silence because there's wind and waves and seagulls, there's rain on the pier above us but there's this silence between us, you can hear it like it's a noise and she's leaning over and she's kissing me. Goldie Shaw is kissing me on my mouth.

Fucking what? I've still got rage so I keep my hands by my side but hers are on my face and then my neck and then we stop. What the fuck? I'm only at the first pier. Not enough hurt to take the rage away.

GOLDIE. Was it one of your poems?

CARL. What?

GOLDIE. Were you shouting one of your poems?

CARL. I don't know what you mean? What poems?

GOLDIE. It's alright, I think it's sound.

CARL. Right. I don't know what you mean.

GOLDIE. Your dad was talking about them.

CARL. What? When?

GOLDIE. He was in the shop on Saturday.

CARL. Your shop? Your mum and dad's shop?

GOLDIE. Yeah he comes in a lot. He buys toys. Have you got a little brother?

CARL. No.

GOLDIE. Oh. Anyway, he was in there on Saturday and he was chatting to my dad and he said that you've got into writing poems about Blackpool.

CARL. What? I haven't.

GOLDIE. I think it's sound Carl, you don't have to –

CARL. I don't. I don't even write poems.

GOLDIE. Your dad told my dad that you do.

CARL. Well they can both fuck off out of my business because I don't write poems.

She laughs – it bursts out of her like affection and embarrassment and excitement.

GOLDIE. Carl!

CARL. What?

GOLDIE. Don't tell my dad to fuck off.

GOLDIE laughs. CARL speaks to the audience.

CARL. And she's laughing. What does she think she's laughing at?

What are you laughing at Goldie Shaw?

She kissed me and now she's laughing in my face, knowing that she's better than me because I'm not as good as her and I write poems and my dad buys toys from her shop, from her cool mum and dad's shop. I'm still carrying this rage, I haven't run far enough and it's her fault, she stopped me, she kissed me, she kissed me and my muscles are starting to feel warm and nice and the rage is coming back, not enough hurt. Second pier. Fuck it. I'm running again. She's shouting behind me, something I can't hear. Something that doesn't land. I need to feel the pain in my lungs, pain in my side and pain in my legs to take all this rage away. I'll deal with it all later.

The noise of rain builds as CARL *runs. He runs and then stops, catches his breath and moves.*

Later that day.

So I write poems. What's wrong with that? They're only songs without music. Kids that write songs are cool. That's not true, that's not true at all. Kids that write songs are geeks and they get bullied and kids that write poems are worse and they get bullied worse and so they should. I'd do the same. I'm gonna be known as the pouf-poem boy or the gayer who writes love poems, not even that, just The Blackpool Gay!

Dad man, what were you thinking? What makes you think that kids like Goldie Shaw and her mates are going to let this stuff slide? Me! Carl! I've got muscles and a shaved head and I'm alright. It's over for me. I can hear them, they're at it now –

Phoning and typing and texting and Skyping.
They don't let stuff like this slide.
They don't, they won't and neither would I,
They shan't, they can't and it's one in the eye,
Cos the cool kids, they-rule kids,

the inside, whereas I'd get angry on the outside and shout and punch the walls. But my dad was the weirdest. His was the weirdest by far. He got into something, like, well, he got into something in a big way. He got into... I wish I could say that it was fighting or drinking, drinking would be good, I could have handled that but he didn't get into drinking, no, he got into – I remember the day I found out.

The scene alters to show this earlier memory.

Dad!

DAD (*off*). Yeah.

CARL. What you doing?

DAD (*off*). Nothing. Why?

CARL. What's that noise?

DAD (*off*). Nothing.

Beat.

I've bought something. Come and have a look.

CARL. So I climbed the stairs.

Somewhere in the space DAD *is in the loft with a small toy train set.* CARL *has had a bad day, the rage has passed but bits of it remain. He climbs the stairs, enters the room and stands still, looking.*

DAD. Do you like it?

CARL. I'm not sure Dad. What's it for?

DAD. It's not for anything Carl. It's for the train to go round and round. I think I like it.

CARL. Are you alright Dad?

DAD. Fine. You?

CARL. Not really, I've had a bad day.

DAD. You going for a run?

CARL. Yeah.

And the caught-between-two-stools kids,
Are just. Left. To die.

Well not me. Fuck that. Not me.

CARL *seamlessly moves into a scene in his kitchen at home*
some weeks later – he is charged and excited and full of
power. When he recites the poem, it's not rehearsed or
thought about – it's coming from within him.

The Infantry – 1st Battalion Duke of Lancasters. Sir! Three
weeks till I go. Sir! Three weeks to get things straight, to sort
things out and to buy some stuff and to do some things and
get everything sorted and cross things off lists and to tell my
dad and to tell my dad and to tell my dad, my dad, my dad,
to tell my dad I'm in –

I'm in. I'm in. I'm fucking well in,
So sure as shit I'm out.
I'm in the forces, the fighting forces and out of this
    broken-down town.

No more bleak bad bus trips,
To the sea front, sick stink social,
And forward to freedom, to fighting freedom,
To power protection and pride.

Gone is the grey, is the grease and the gloom,
The going-dull gloss of God's country,
And here's to the heights, to the illustrious sights, of
    foreign excitement and glory.

So goodbye to the bleak British backwater boredom,
And hello to being the best, to guns and drums and
    fighting fitness,
To getting ahead of the rest.

All signed, sent back and sorted. It's too late now anyway,
what can he say? It's signed, sent back and sorted.

I'm in, I'm in – to tell my dad I'm in.

I was twelve when my mum died and we all went a bit weird.
Me and Uncle Charles were like opposites. He'd come round
quite a lot and just sit and be quiet and fat and get all tense on

DAD. Go on then.

CARL. It's cool Dad. I like it.

DAD. Yeah. See you later.

This scene dissolves and CARL *is back in the present talking to the audience.*

CARL. Trains. Like, little toy ones that go round a track. What does that mean? What is he if he's addicted to playing with trains that go round a track? Like a kid? At least that's what it used to be, a little track. It's not just a little track any more. No. He's converted the loft. He's built a land. He's built countryside for his trains, it's got a big hill with a tunnel going through it. And they toot. Seriously. Like to tell the little plastic men that don't move and that aren't real to get out of the way. He's got loads of stuff, like about fifteen trains and some things that they pull, with coal in, he's got signals and crossings that come down over roads to stop the cars that don't move. He's got sheep! Plastic sheep to go in his plastic fields. And he's always at it. He lives up there. Nights usually. So he can turn their lights on.

Three weeks to tell him I'm in. Tell him I'm in, tell him I'm in. He's gonna – he'll be alright. He has to be. Cos I'm not having Blackpool printed on my bones. No chance. No skeleton of rock for me, no town-printed marrow, no sugar-pink tibia and fibula, with blue-inked Blackpool at my core. Bollocks. I'm doing it. No I'm not.

Shit. I could just sack it off and not go. And do what? Become a poet in Blackpool? No chance. Do it. Do it. Do it. I'm up, I'm out the kitchen, I'm up the stairs, banister, treads, into the loft.

Somewhere in the space DAD *is in the loft with many more trains – there is a hillside and a tunnel and several trains going round several tracks.*

Alright Dad?

DAD. Alright there Carl? How are you son?

CARL. Good. Good. What you up to?

DAD. Trains.

CARL. Yeah. Apart from the trains Dad, what are you up to?

DAD. Nothing. What's up son?

CARL. I got you this.

> CARL *hands him a box. It's a train.* DAD *looks at it.*

DAD. Oh. Carl. That's grand. Hey look at that. Thank you son.
That's just brilliant, that is just... I'll introduce her this
evening for the lights, see what they're like. Lovely that
Carl, thank you.

CARL. I'm going away Dad.

DAD. Going away? What do you mean?

CARL. I'm going away.

DAD. Where to?

CARL. Catterick.

DAD. What for?

CARL. The army.

DAD. Oh. Oh.

CARL. I've signed up.

DAD. No. Really?

CARL. Are you alright Dad?

DAD. Yeah.

> *Silence.*

> Thanks for the train son. I'll look after it.

CARL. No worries Dad.

DAD. Carl?

CARL. Yeah.

DAD. Why?

CARL. To see the world Dad. To get out.

DAD. Right.

Blackpool town centre forms somewhere in the space. It's three weeks prior. An Army recruitment stall with soldiers in full regalia handing out information. CARL is in two worlds for a moment until he is intrigued by the stall and leaves the home scene to dissolve.

RECRUITING OFFICER. Do you want to see the world?

CARL. What?

RECRUITING OFFICER. Do you want to see the world?

CARL. Don't know. Yeah. I suppose so. One day.

RECRUITING OFFICER. How old are you?

CARL (*to the audience*). I was in town and they had a stall out – the Army. I just went and had a look, picked up some leaflets and had a look and this recruiting officer just said:

RECRUITING OFFICER. Do you want to see the world?

CARL. Yeah.

RECRUITING OFFICER. Do you like it here in Blackpool?

CARL. No.

RECRUITING OFFICER. Do you have any qualifications?

CARL. No.

RECRUITING OFFICER. Are you in full-time education at the moment?

CARL. No.

RECRUITING OFFICER. Are you in full-time employment at the moment?

CARL. No.

RECRUITING OFFICER. Do you want a job where you get qualifications while you work? Does that sound like something you'd be interested in? Does that suit you more than studying at a college? Are you more adept to practical than academic pursuits?

CARL. Where would I go?

RECRUITING OFFICER. That depends.

CARL. On what?

RECRUITING OFFICER. That depends on what you want to
do, what you want to be.

CARL. What can I be?

RECRUITING OFFICER. You can be anything you want to be
son. Come and have a seat.

*The recruiting scene dissolves into darkness. Somewhere else
in the space* DAD *is stood, helpless, readying himself to say
goodbye.*

DAD. So are you all packed?

CARL *turns and is now in the scene with* DAD.

CARL. Yeah. Everything's ready.

DAD. I got you something.

CARL. Yeah? What is it?

DAD. I got you it because I thought you might need it.

DAD *hands it to him.*

It's a whistle. I thought you could keep it with you. You never
know, it might come in handy one day. You might need it.

CARL. Yeah. Cheers Dad.

DAD. That's a good one. Real, genuine guard's whistle.
Designed to be heard over the noise of a diesel train so you
should be alright with that one. Do you know how it works?

CARL. What? Yeah you blow in it. Are you for real Dad?

DAD. It's the vortex. A whistle makes a smooth flow of air split
and when it splits it creates a turbulent vortex and it's that
that makes the air vibrate and that's the noise. It's a turbulent
vortex in whistles, not a forced one like you'd imagine. Do
you know what a turbulent vortex is?

CARL. No. No Dad I don't. It's cool Dad thanks.

Pause.

DAD. They don't give you one you know?

CARL. No?

DAD. I checked.

CARL. Right.

DAD. I phoned them up and asked what equipment you get as an infantry soldier. You don't get a whistle.

CARL. Right. I'll keep it with me. I will, I'll take it everywhere, you know, just in case.

I'll be in touch and I'll be back on my long-weekend break in a few weeks.

DAD. Six.

CARL. Six.

Silence.

Right then. Look after yourself Dad.

DAD. You too Carl son.

The DAD *scene disappears.* CARL *is alone and active. He talks to the audience.*

CARL. Coach from Blackpool to Leeds, bus from Leeds to Catterick and I walked the rest of the way. Same rain, new streets.

I was early so I walked around and looked around, you know? I felt new, with my backpack on in the rain, watching people get up and go to work and run to their cars to get out of the rain or bring their milk in off the doorstep and look for a moment at the bloke with his hood up and backpack on watching them from their garden wall. I just stood there in the driving rain and I'm thinking that this is North Yorkshire. North Yorkshire. Where is that? I don't know where it is but I know where it isn't. It isn't anywhere near the Appletons and Uncle Charles and Goldie Shaw and her fuckin' laughing in my face. This is what life's about, getting out and getting on. Seein' the world I am, seein' the world starts now.

SERGEANT STOKES *appears*.

There's about forty of us, not all lads but mostly, in this hall in the barracks in Catterick. Everyone looks dry but I'm piss-wet through from the walk but that's alright. I'm stood in this hall and there's like a puddle around me, it's all dripped off me and I can see it rivering off along the floor in different directions, touching the guy's feet in front of me, like connecting us –

SERGEANT STOKES. Good morning. My name is Sergeant William Stokes. I'm not one for big speeches, I am simply here to welcome you to the British Army and to what can be the most exciting, important and fulfilling career choice you will ever make. You will become specialists. You will become experts, you will learn from masters of their craft. You will become better than you ever thought you could be. I am here to welcome you to your future. Take a moment to look around this room. Should you successfully complete the following twenty-four weeks to the standard the British Army expects then, these are the people that will be with you for the rest of your lives. Lifelong relationships are forged in the armed forces by the very nature of what we do. Trust is essential. Be under no illusions, this is a dangerous job, now more than ever and the people that you are standing with here will be watching over you when you're sleeping, they will be keeping you safe. Believe me, after this training course these people will be with you in the most extreme places imaginable and you will rely on them when you need them. Take a look. This is your family now. You will look after them and they will look after you and together we will defend this country. That's it. Let's go to work.

CARL *bursts into action. The next three weeks are played out in this poem – as many of the activities that he describes as possible should be physicalised and acted out by* CARL *during the poem.*

CARL.

> Up now, out there, stand here and listen hard. Eyes front,
> shoulders back, chest out and on your guard. Always.
> All days are like this. You're. Not. Going. To. Like.
> This.

> Sign here, take these, wear this and cut that. Eat then,
> sleep there, wash here and shut that. Gob. Job to do
> son. That's all. Here's your gun.

> Run up, duck down, cover over and out of sight. Eyes
> open, mouth shut. Work heavy and sleep light. Tonight.
> Tomorrow. And always. All days are war days.

> Watch me, chase him, shoot there and kill that. Inform
> him, ignore them, hide here and follow that. Route.
> Shoot to kill son. Don't. Let. Me down son.

I love it. It's top. I am loving it, I am really properly loving
it. It's hard and it's cold. I mean fuck me, next time I join the
Army I'm gonna do it in summer when you can run in the
sun. But I love it. I'm free and me. Free and me and running.
Rain or frost or in the middle of the night, we run.

CARL *starts to run. As he runs he is handed uniform and a
backpack and equipment. He is becoming a soldier, he's
becoming constricted.*

I want a little bit more today though, today feels like if I was
at home I'd be in a rage, I'd be biting if I was at home today,
but today I'm here. I'm here and fuckin' Bilko's next to me.

Not today Bilko mate, not today.

Somewhere in the space BILKO *is running too. It's beautiful
and synchronised and rhythmic. As the scene progresses it
become more than running, it's hard and fast and aggressive.*

His name's Tony Wilkinson but we called him Wilko and
then Bilko. He's in my barracks, he's in my dorm, he's in the
bed next to me, he's one of my mates. We do this thing. It's
meant to be all men together on the runs. Like a unit, leave
no man behind and all that. A group, a team, all in it together.
And that's wicked, I love it, but me and Bilko we've got this

thing, like, we race each other. Just me and him and if you get called back to help someone, if someone needs you, then that's all part of it. Tough shit, you go back, you lose, Bilko wins. It's a laugh. But I'm raging a little bit today and I want this run for me. I can feel a bit in my chest and in my side but I want a proper burn. I want that wicked nasty, nerve-breaker one in the deep of my spine, that proper nasty twinge, I want that one. But I can't get it going with Bilko playing *Chariots of Fire* next to me. Today I'm helping no one and I'm not racing Bilko, today it's me.

BILKO. Going for it today Jackson.

CARL (*ignores him*). Block him out. Get some good hurt, got some in my knee, build it, stamp that leg, get the knee, knee, knee, knee, get it, get it, get it.

BILKO. On a mission big boy? Don't get all special about it.

CARL (*continuing to ignore him*). Shut up prick I'm trying to get some hurt here. Get that spine one, get that spine one, get-that-spine-one.

BILKO. Not speaking Jackson? You not my friend today? Come on, let it out or I might cry.

CARL (*ignoring him*). Chest is good and burning, real hurt in there, nice proper fire in there going strong. Knee is making me bite. Come on, more, hate it, hate it, break it.

BILKO. Come on Jackson, don't be a girl.

CARL (*ignoring him*). Shut up prick. Get hurting and block him out.

BILKO. Jackson.

CARL (*ignoring him*). Shut up I can't concentrate.

BILKO. Jackson for fuck's sake, slow down.

CARL (*ignoring him*). SHUT UP, SHUT UP, SHUT UP.

BILKO. Jackson. Jackson. Jackson you prick, you're gonna get us into trouble.

They stop running. CARL *grabs* BILKO. *We feel his true anger boiling. He lets go at him.*

CARL. FUCK OFF THEN PRICK. FUCK OFF AND LEAVE ME TO IT!

(To himself.) Nnnaaaggghhh. It's gone. No chest now, knee is filling up with warm, good fluids to take the pain away, my fists are like rock balls and I'm staring him down, we've stopped, everyone else is running and we've stopped and I'm staring him down and I think I'm gonna knock his bastard, little stupid head off, I'm gonna totally splay this prick –

Somewhere in the space the CORPORAL *appears.*

CORPORAL. Get your fucking legs moving. What the hell in shit's name have you two stopped for? Jackson take your temper over there. NOW! Move! Wilkinson, get running. Go! Move, move, move. Now then Jackson. Just me and you now Jackson. Feeling frisky today are we?

BILKO *exits.* CARL *switches between talking to the audience and addressing the* CORPORAL.

CARL. And I'm charged, too charged, it's a massive rage and I can't hold on to it.

CORPORAL. I'm sorry, I just asked you a question Jackson, now this is your last and final chance to answer it. Are you feeling frisky today?

CARL. Spitting all bad, early morning, nasty shit breath all over me? Just one quick jerk and my head's in his face. Bosh. Blood and bone. Just one. Do it. Crack. Do it.

CORPORAL. Answer me Jackson. Are you feeling frisky today?

CARL. Yes.

CORPORAL. What did you just say?

CARL. Yes sir!

CORPORAL. Well I don't care. I don't care and you need to care about what I care about. Is that clear?

CARL. No it isn't. Just do it. Properly destroy his face. Break his tight little skin-and-bone ridge for him. Do it. Do it. Do it Carl.

Yes sir!

CORPORAL. These men are your bastard brothers. Are you going to be the one to let them down? There's always one selfish little prick out for himself. Is that you Jackson?

CARL. Gonna do it. Gonna do it. Can't hold on –

CORPORAL. Answer me Jackson!

CARL. No sir! That's not me sir!

CORPORAL. Damn right boy. You think this is frisky? You haven't even started. Now I don't care what kind of lovers' tiff you and Wilkinson had this morning. You swallow that shit, you dig deep, you bite down hard and you keep on running. Not for yourself, not for your gay little temper, not for me but for that group of men who need you to be in control. Does that make sense?

CARL. Yes sir.

CORPORAL. Show me.

CARL. What?

CORPORAL. WHAT?

CARL. What sir?

CORPORAL. Show me you're in control.

CARL. What now?

CORPORAL. RUN!

CARL. YES SIR!

> (*To audience*.) So I did. I got running. I'm not gonna be the one. I'm not the one, I'm like everyone else me, nothing different here. Stone-cold strong and fighting hard. Just like the rest.

> *Back at the barracks* – BILKO *appears as if just out of the shower.*

BILKO. Alright Jackson?

CARL. Yeah. You?

BILKO. Yeah, knockout, I could run it again.

> BILKO *exits.*

CARL. He didn't even mention it. That's pretty sound that. I'd have had it out with him I think. Maybe. Maybe I wouldn't. Not now, not any more.

A beat.

I got a postcard from Uncle Charles. He couldn't phone or text like a normal bloke could he? No, idiot Uncle Charles sends a postcard with thirteen Blackpool words on it.

From somewhere in the space – UNCLE CHARLES *reads what he has written.*

UNCLE CHARLES. Your dad's grown a beard again. You're gonna have to come home. Charles.

UNCLE CHARLES *exits.*

CARL. Fuck that. No. I'm out of there and beyond. Fuck Dad with his beard.

Kenya now.

Lights change to bright heat.

Kenya. Africa. I'm in Kenya. I can't believe it. Who does that? Who pays you to go to Africa with all of your closest mates? The big-boy British Army, that's who. I've never even been on a plane and now I'm in Kenya. It's hot though and it's bad. It's a bad place Nairobi you can just tell. We're on some barracks just outside the city but when we're in Nairobi you can feel it, they hate us. They hate us because of what we've got. Not money and cars and electronic stuff, I mean shoes, they hate us because we've got shoes and they haven't. Not everyone, some people like us, not many though. Some of the lads get a bit heavy with it. Taking the piss, goading the locals, getting them all frisky. I don't get involved.

CARL *starts to run. It's rhythmic and solid and different, it doesn't build or get harder, it flows and it's strong.*

We're here to train and to run and to shoot and to get used to extremes. Hot in the day, really hot but you take it, you run, but now we're not just running like we were in Catterick in winter, we're running together in a different place a hot place that doesn't look like anywhere else in my head and we're running towards things.

Somewhere in the space BILKO *is running. They run together, synchronised and rhythmic. The noise of their feet is amplified somehow. It builds. It drives them on.*

We're running towards things together, strong legs and it's double hot but that doesn't matter, you take it, you grow to like the heat, you grow to need the heat, it's weird without it. You miss it when it's not there. Like burning inside you hot. Like your bones are being cooked and they're the hottest part of you and you piss your pants because of all the water and then it's night and the cold comes. So cold that you feel it hard, harder than the heat, it bites you and you cramp and you shake, you really shake, so you run, you run at night to stop the shaking and you watch the horizon for the sun. You don't sleep, you just shiver and you just run and watch the horizon for the sun and the heat that it brings, just a little bit of heat, just enough to… but it's never just a little bit, it's never a little bit in Kenya. Extremes. Too hot, too cold, too hot, too cold, too much not enough. Kenya. You take it. You take it all.

They run and the rhythm of their feet builds and builds until it's a beat, until it's a noise. Until it becomes the beat to music. As they run they have some of their equipment and uniform changed and replaced by other members of the company. Their previously clean and new uniform and equipment is replaced by older, worn and damaged stuff. Time passes. They grow and feel more comfortable in these clothes and holding their guns. The music plays throughout.

Suddenly the music stops. CARL *is alone in light.*

Kenya hurt me. It hurt us all. Kenya hurt, Germany was boring and Cyprus was a holiday but I'm through all that, we all are. We toughed it out together. 1st Duke of Lancasters. Infantry. That's me. That's us. We fight, we win, we carry on. I've seen some stuff. I've seen some stuff, some heavy stuff. Not just Army stuff, you know? Some bad stuff. I've seen some bad-boy British stuff. Fuck it. We fight, we win, we carry on. Carry on.

CARL *marches as he recites the next poem. It's rigid and tight and controlled like a machine.*

Say goodbye, you've come a long way,
You're doing your country proud.
And now it's time to take the next step,
So say 'Yes sir' nice and loud.

You don't have a choice; you're coming with us,
You were selected for being so good.
You're strong and quick and your aim is top-five,
And you don't mind the sight of fresh blood.

It's not going to be pretty, I'm not going to lie,
We're going to a godawful place,
But we're going for Britain, for Queen and country,
So do it with pride on your face.

Now go back up north and see your family,
Show them you've turned out just fine.
Show them with pride the man you've become,
Cos you won't be seeing them for some time.

Somewhere else in the space CARL*'s* DAD *is sat in the kitchen in Blackpool. He has grown a beard.*

DAD. Sit down son. Sit down then. Good to see you, good to see you.

CARL *talks to the audience. His* DAD *busies himself in the kitchen.*

CARL. When my mum died my dad grew a beard. No one mentioned it at first. But it stayed and he looked different. Like he was trying to be different. I don't know. It wasn't a big deal, he shaved it off when he got his first train. It wasn't a big deal. But now he's grown another one it feels like a bit more of a deal.

DAD. Good to see you Carl.

CARL. How're you doing Dad?

DAD. Now then. Do you want a cup of tea?

CARL. No ta Dad I'm alright.

DAD. Sure?

CARL. Yeah.

DAD. You look different.

CARL. Yeah? So do you.

DAD. People are proud of you Carl.

CARL. What people?

DAD. Everyone.

CARL. Dad you don't know that.

DAD. I do.

CARL. You don't.

DAD. You don't know, you're not here.

CARL. I don't need to be. People from Blackpool don't get proud, they get jealous and pissed off and they take the piss.

DAD. Not true. Not true. That is not true.

CARL. I've seen it.

DAD. You've seen nothing, you're a boy.

CARL. You've seen nothing, you don't leave the bastard house man.

DAD. I do.

CARL. You don't. You're fucking cracked-up Dad.

DAD. Do you remember when I slapped you and you cried Carl?

CARL. No.

DAD. You do. I did. I slapped you and you cried and I'll do it again. Big soldier now are you? Talking to people like that. I can still do it.

CARL. Alright Dad.

DAD. No it isn't. No it isn't. Do you want a cup of tea?

CARL. No ta Dad I'm fine.

DAD. When are you coming home?

CARL. I am home.

DAD. I mean properly.

CARL. I'm not Dad. This is it from now on.

DAD. I thought you were just doing the training.

CARL. I passed. I passed ages ago. I'm in and training for combat now Dad.

DAD. You used your whistle yet?

CARL. No. Not yet.

DAD. Keep it with you though. Keep it with you. You know? Keep it with you.

CARL. I do.

DAD. Do you want a cup of –

Loud dance music cuts him off. Somewhere else in the space GOLDIE SHAW *is dancing. We watch her dance. She looks free and happy.* DAD *exits and the kitchen scene dissolves into darkness, we are with* GOLDIE *now. She dances.* CARL *joins her. She sees him.*

GOLDIE. Carl? Carl Jackson?

CARL. Goldie? Goldie, how are you?

GOLDIE. Fuckin' hell I thought it was you. Carl Jackson as I live and breathe. What are you doing here?

CARL. I'm just seeing some of the lads.

GOLDIE. How long are you staying?

CARL. Few days, maybe a week.

GOLDIE. Bloody hell, Carl Jackson, how long have you been away for now?

CARL. Dunno.

GOLDIE. Piss off.

CARL. What?

GOLDIE. It's eleven months.

CARL. Yeah?

GOLDIE. Yeah. You left a hole.

CARL. Yeah?

GOLDIE. Yeah, a bit. Look it's loud in here do you want to go outside?

CARL. Yeah, sure.

The music fades to a low thump in the background. Outside.

GOLDIE. Fuckin' Blackpool.

CARL. Yeah I know, shit isn't it?

GOLDIE. Is it?

CARL. Yeah.

GOLDIE. Fair enough.

CARL. What?

GOLDIE. Nothing.

CARL. What?

GOLDIE. I just don't think it's that shit that's all.

CARL. No?

GOLDIE. No.

CARL. Right. I do.

GOLDIE. Yeah. I get that.

Pause.

You look different y'know.

CARL. People keep saying that.

GOLDIE. Yeah? Well they're right.

CARL. Right. Well, so do you.

GOLDIE (*laughing*). Fuck off Carl.

CARL. What?

GOLDIE. No I don't.

CARL. Okay.

GOLDIE. You're being all fly, Carl.

CARL. Am I?

GOLDIE. Yeah.

CARL. Okay.

Pause.

Their silences aren't uncomfortable or challenging, they are natural and charged with potential. They glance at each other, sometimes together sometimes when the other isn't looking, sometimes when the other chooses not to look.

How's everything here then?

GOLDIE. What do you care, you think it's shit?

CARL. So it's not shit then?

GOLDIE. No.

CARL. No?

GOLDIE. No. It's not.

CARL. What makes it not shit?

GOLDIE. What makes it not shit? What kind of grammar is that then? I thought you wrote poems.

CARL. Fuck off.

GOLDIE. Don't tell me to fuck off Carl Jackson.

CARL. Fuck off.

They smile.

GOLDIE. You don't like it do you?

CARL. What?

GOLDIE. Someone talking about your poems.

CARL. I don't care.

GOLDIE. Bullshit, yeah you do.

CARL. No I don't, I'm on-top.

GOLDIE. Say one then.

CARL. Say one what?

GOLDIE. A poem.

CARL. No.

GOLDIE. Say one to me now. Why not?

CARL. Because I don't even write poems.

GOLDIE. I thought you didn't care. I thought you were on-top. Say one.

CARL. No.

GOLDIE. Mary had a little lamb…

CARL. Piss off Goldie.

GOLDIE. What? I don't care. I'll say one.

> Mary had a little lamb…

CARL. Shut up.

GOLDIE. No.

> Mary had a little lamb she tied it to a pylon,
> A thousand volts went up its arse,
> And turned its wool to Nylon.

CARL. You're not funny.

GOLDIE. Yes I am. I am a funny girl Carl. Just because you're training to kill people and you look different it doesn't mean that I'm not funny. That is a funny poem, you could learn something from that.

CARL. Whatever.

Pause.

GOLDIE. So have you shot anyone yet?

CARL. No, have I fuck.

GOLDIE. Sorry, I'm only asking.

CARL. I'm still in training aren't I?

GOLDIE. I don't know do I? Still in training after eleven months, how long does it take?

CARL. Ages. There's different kinds.

GOLDIE. Either that or you're just a bit shit.

CARL. I haven't been in theatre yet. If I'd shot anyone it'd mean that I'd shot one of my own, which would mean that I am more than a bit shit.

GOLDIE. And you're not?

CARL. No.

GOLDIE. Just us then.

CARL. What?

GOLDIE. Nothing.

Pause.

Would you?

CARL. What?

GOLDIE. Shoot someone?

CARL. Yeah, I reckon.

GOLDIE. Yeah? Fair enough.

CARL. You would too. Anyone would.

GOLDIE. Oh, I know I would Carl Jackson. In fact I might have to borrow that Uzi of yours if my old man gives me any more grief.

CARL. He's alright your dad isn't he?

GOLDIE. Yeah, he's alright. I still see yours.

CARL. Yeah?

GOLDIE. Yeah, from time to time. We chat y'know?

CARL. Yeah? Good luck with that.

GOLDIE. You're at it again.

CARL. What?

GOLDIE. Being all fly.

CARL. Sorry.

GOLDIE. So what's it like then? Really.

CARL. It's better than here.

GOLDIE. I'm not going to tell you again Carl.

CARL. Tell me what?

GOLDIE. I live here. You might have jumped ship and found a better beach to play on but Blackpool is my home so stop saying it's shit.

CARL. Alright, calm down.

GOLDIE. No. Blackpool's not shit Carl, you just choose to see it that way. You used to live on that Pleasure Beach when you were a kid. Fuckin' smiles wider than the front. I watched you then too.

CARL. I'm not a kid any more though am I?

GOLDIE. Clearly.

CARL. I'm out of here Goldie and it's bigger and better and... I'm better, I breathe better. I do. Free and me. That's it.

GOLDIE. Have you got a Pleasure Beach though?

CARL. The biggest.

GOLDIE. Stay safe out there Superfly. We don't want you tripping over your shoelace and shooting yourself in the head now. It happens, I've seen it on YouTube.

CARL. I'll try.

GOLDIE. Good.

Silence. It lasts.

Are you going to kiss me then or what?

CARL. You what?

GOLDIE. Bloody hell, I hope you're not in the Signals Carl Jackson or else we're all fucked.

She kisses him. It's youthful and hungry and full of true love. The music builds. It's loud and then cuts out as CARL *suddenly breaks away from the kiss.*

CARL. Afghanistan!!!

CARL *is in bright light. It's midday, it's hot. Afghanistan.*

Afghanistan. I fuckin' love it. It's hot and weird and beautiful and scary as hell and I properly, seriously love it. This is it. This is tight and nasty and dusty and not good.

Everything is dusty, like it gets everywhere. You get up in the morning and all you can hear is people blowing their noses. Dust and sand and heat but that's alright because we're in Afghanistan and it's proper war. Afghanistan man. You can feel it all the time, everyone's double prepared all professional and wanting some. Training's over and it's time to get involved. It's time to get serious, it's time to get properly, heavily ready for the front – What the fuck are you doing?

Elsewhere in the space BILKO *is stripped down to his underwear and is lying on the ground.*

BILKO. Getting a tan.

CARL. Are you for real? We're in Helmand man.

BILKO. So.

CARL. So we're meant to be at war and you're sunbathing.

BILKO. A tan's a tan wherever you are Squirt and I look good brown.

I look very good brown.

CARL. What are you meant to be doing?

BILKO. Cleaning the shitters.

CARL. Right?

BILKO. I got an Abdul to do it.

CARL. Which one?

BILKO. That happy one with the fucked-up teeth. He's alright. Chill out and get your top off, we've got half an hour before we get called in so make the most of it Squirt.

After a beat CARL *does.*

Hey. Have you been working out?

CARL. Shut up.

He lies down and soaks up the sun.

Do you reckon we'll get out today?

BILKO. No.

CARL. Why not?

BILKO. Because I've heard it's all kicking off next week. Big deployment. Us and two Czech companies are going north, suited and booted Squirt. You ready for it?

CARL. Yeah. You?

BILKO. Not really.

CARL. What do you mean? We're here to fight man. Queen and country and all that shit.

BILKO. Yeah, I've been thinking about that and I've concluded that I'm more of a lover not a fighter. It's what I'm good at.

CARL. What you're good at is talking rubbish.

BILKO. Are you flirting with me Squirt?

CARL. You'd know about it if I was.

BILKO. Stop it you're giving me a Tim Henman.

CARL. What's a Tim Henman?

BILKO. An unexpected semi. Put your top back on before I blow.

CARL. Seriously though, you up for it?

BILKO. It's why I joined.

CARL. You reckon we'll see some stuff?

BILKO. If we're ever gonna see anything it's here and now. Some poor bastards spend twenty years kicking their own arses around every base the British Army's got and they never see anything. We did a year and a half of running and now we've hit the jackpot. It's hot here boy and I'm not just talking about the sun, although that is hot and I'm trying to get a tan so shut up.

CARL. Yeah. It'll be alright, we know what we're doing.

BILKO. Are you getting twitchy?

CARL. No.

BILKO. Don't get gay on me. Strong as they come now.

CARL. Always.

BILKO. Yeah?

CARL. Yeah.

BILKO. Good. Now shut up, I'm concentrating.

CARL. On what?

BILKO. On my fuckin' tan!

CARL *moves to address the audience.* BILKO *exits.*

CARL. We did go out that day. Just for a few hours and then back to base but it was enough. It was enough to know that it's twisted here. It's bad and it's quiet and it's twisted. We thought they hated us in Kenya. In Kenya they just wanted us to piss off home, to leave them alone, but it was noisy and normal there. These fuckers are quiet and cold and they want us dead and buried in their sand-land. You can see it in their eyes and yeah I'm twitchy and if Bilko says he isn't then he's even more full of crap than I had him down for. It's work though. It's work, busy as fuck and strong as they come. We fight, we win, we carry on. Always. We fight, we win, we carry on.

Snap into the following week. Night. CARL *is lying down pointing a rifle. Elsewhere in the space* BILKO *is doing the same. They speak to each other quietly through microphone headsets. This is played out in the space.*

Shit man. Shit. Fucking hell, I don't like this, I'm not sure about this, this is a bit messed up, it's a bit strong this, it's a bit much man. Bilko. Bilko are you there?

BILKO. Shut the fuck up and get on with it.

CARL. I can't.

BILKO. Of course you can. Do it.

CARL. I can't.

BILKO. You can and you bloody will boy. It's you, so just shut up and do it.

CARL. Shit. I can't.

BILKO. Do it. It's him or us.

CARL. But he's asleep.

BILKO. So? Good.

CARL. It's not right.

BILKO. He's Taliban man. Fact. Slot him or I'll slot you, right here right now.

CARL. Yeah?

BILKO. I'm not joking Carl.

CARL. I'd snap you in two Bilko! I'd knock you bandy so get off my back.

BILKO. Shoot the fucker then and I will. Shoot. Carl, just do it now. Do it. Do it Carl. PULL THAT TRIGGER NOW!

Somewhere in the space GOLDIE *emerges in light.*

GOLDIE. Carl?

CARL. Ah, fuck this.

He shoots. Simultaneously BILKO *cracks open a can of beer. We are immediately back at the base. It's later.* BILKO *is sat.* CARL *is stood, he is playing with the whistle.* GOLDIE *is gone.*

BILKO. Now then Squirt, you've made me a very proud man today. A very proud man.

CARL. Shut up Bilko man, it was only one kill.

BILKO. One kill? One kill, he says. That was a stone-cold execution chap and he didn't know a thing about it. Civilised, a very civilised way of getting your first score.

CARL. If anyone hears you talking like that you're in major-league trouble man.

BILKO. Shut up Blue Peter, everyone talks like it, just not when those fuckin' reporters are about that's all. Seriously though are you alright?

CARL. Yeah, knockout.

BILKO. It's your job.

CARL. I know what my job is.

BILKO. I'm just checking that your head's okay.

CARL. It's sound. You just look after your end.

BILKO. Alright then. Fair enough. We made ground because of it though Squirt. You start questioning yourself and just remember that we made good ground because of it.

CARL moves to the audience. Out of focus, BILKO exits. CARL is still, his movements are constricted. He plays with the whistle.

CARL. I need to run. I think I need to go home and run a properly long Blackpool beach run in the rain. Tears on your face in the rain and she's laughing but it's raining hard and you try not to but you can still hear her. Even out here you can hear her. See her sometimes too, if you try. No running in Afghanistan though, no running out here, it's tight and tense and I need a proper nasty spinal twinge for a couple of hours on rainy old Blackpool Beach. Good old, bad old Blackpool. Wrapped up though. Wrapped up and trapped up with a gun... and the sun and a vision... a vision... a vision of what I've done. I just need to run. Just need to stay focused. It's work, it's just a job, a job with a wage and a wage is a cage. Seeing the world I am. Seeing it all now. Seeing the proper lot.

Somewhere else in the space DAD *is sat in the kitchen in Blackpool.* GOLDIE SHAW *is with him. They take the focus. During this section* CARL *sits and watches them on the fringes of the scene. It is a dream or a fantasy or a homesick wish.*

GOLDIE. Your beard's coming along.

DAD. Yeah.

GOLDIE. You gonna keep it?

DAD. Don't know.

GOLDIE. Tea?

DAD. No ta.

GOLDIE. Sure? I'm having one.

DAD. Yeah, okay then. Two sugars.

GOLDIE. So you're having one then?

DAD. Yeah go on.

GOLDIE. You're sure now because you did this last time –

DAD. They're going to kill him.

Beat.

GOLDIE. He'll be alright George.

DAD. They're going to kill him.

GOLDIE. You don't know that.

DAD. I do. They will, they're going to kill him.

GOLDIE. Stop saying that George. He'll be alright.

DAD. You don't know what he's like.

GOLDIE. I do.

DAD. I gave him a whistle.

GOLDIE. I know.

DAD. Did he tell you?

GOLDIE. No. You did.

DAD. I know I did, I just thought – Do you know what a turbulent vortex is?

GOLDIE. Go on.

DAD. It's energy. It's like a tornado, that's a vortex. It's just energy. Wild, natural, self-propelling energy that can't stop itself once it's started. It breaks things. It just breaks things, it can't help it, it just breaks things and keeps going until it's exhausted itself. Until it's ruined itself of all its energy, until there's nothing left, until there's nothing left at all to give. Or, and this is the more probable outcome, until something else stops it.

Somewhere else in the space CARL *is in Afghanistan. As he takes the focus the Blackpool scene dissolves into darkness. He is drowsy and sluggish and seems older. The poetry doesn't come as easily now.*

CARL. Summer's gone. It's still hot though. Bilko's not happy because we're too busy to sunbathe. It's getting very heavy out here. Too heavy to carry sometimes. We haven't lost anyone yet but we will. You hear of it all the time. If it's not a Brit then it's one of the Yanks or Norwegian lads who've taken a hit. We've got a load of local boys with us but they're just idiots, we try and train them but they don't wanna know, they just stand up and fire and they get shot all the time. What can you do? You've got to look after your own first don't you?

Beat.

We don't sleep much here. Too much has happened. Too much is always happening. It's always happening.

You can hear it all the time,

Shouts and shots and screaming fear, like it's on you, like it's in you, like it's really fuckin' near.

It can happen any time. Any time. Anyone could be Taliban. Anyone could be Taliban. Taliban. Taliban. I don't even know what that means.

I'm up to fifteen now. Fifteen kills. Piss-easy. Put a face on it and fire. It's the best way. They don't hurt when I kill them. I'm good. I make sure it doesn't hurt. I take pride in that. Got to be proud of something I suppose. I don't sleep much me, I never have. Fuckin' Uncle Charles, what's he up to now? Proper Blackpool that bloke, it's printed on his rock like the bones. Like the bones you get on the beach. In the sand. I don't need sleep me, because there's thunder in my blood. Thunder in my blood these days. Thunder.

Gunfire. Time moves forward. CARL is sat on the floor of a bombed-out house, scared and alone and totally exhausted. Deep in a combat zone he is holding on. He is holding an Army ready-to-eat meal. We hear heavy gunfire and shouting coming from outside the house. CARL is talking to himself now, not to the audience. He is trying to make sense of things.

I should want this. I really should want this but... Fuck it come on.

He tries to write a poem but it won't come. He is beginning to break.

We'd march for a day and a night and a day,
Through broken-down... through broken-down... we'd –

Erm – I should want this. I should be able to eat this. Fuck's sake, c'mon Carl.

Through broken-down landscapes and shattered old
     towns... through...
The odd frightened face would watch our way,
Praying we don't turn... don't turn... we don't turn
     round...

Tears start to come but he fights them back.

I can't make them rhyme any more.

I should want this... I should be able to eat this.

I can't.

I'm on top.

But still we wouldn't turn round.

He pushes himself to focus on the poem.

> No pain in my feet, no pain in my knees,
> This three-stone backpack isn't getting me down,
> The cold rain that's pouring isn't getting me wet and I
>   promise I won't turn round.

He begins to break again.

> Because to turn round would... to turn round...

Nah, it's gone... c'mon... nah it's over, it's gone... I'm done. I can't do it. I need to eat but I can't do it. I can't do it, I won't do it, you can't make me but I will. I will. You know I always will.

He's on the very edge. Summoned by his imagination
GOLDIE *appears next to him.*

GOLDIE. Are you alright Carl?

CARL. No. I can't eat this. I should want this... it's chocolate pudding and chocolate sauce... and I can't... I should want this Goldie... I've... March on... I must march on, I'm meant to be able to march on but I'm done in... Chocolate Goldie.

Are you alright Goldie? Are you cracking on and stuff?

GOLDIE. I'm alright, ta. You know me Carl.

CARL. No flies on you Goldie Shaw... Do you want this? It's chocolate pudding in chocolate sauce. Go on, have it, I can't eat it.

She doesn't move.

GOLDIE. Are you okay Carl?

CARL. Been in this bombed-out house for thirteen hours y'know? Been fighting the Taliban across the field. They've got RPGs and Russian rifles, good ones, proper good big ones Goldie and I'm... I'm really fuckin'... I dunno, thirteen hours, we don't sleep and I can't eat this. They don't rhyme any more. I can't make my poems rhyme.

GOLDIE. So you do write poems then?

CARL. I used to.

GOLDIE. I knew it. Thank you.

CARL. What for?

GOLDIE. I don't know, for being bigger than this.

CARL. Thirteen hours though Goldie.

He offers her the meal.

Do you want this? If you press the button it heats up. I've been thinking about pressing the button. I've thought about it a lot.

GOLDIE. What's happened Carl?

CARL. Stuff. Stuff that puts thunder in your blood.

GOLDIE. That was always there Carl Jackson.

CARL. Yeah... always. I'm thinking about pressing it. I'm going to press it. I'm going to press it and finish it and y'know, force it down my neck. If I puke I puke at least it's something in't it? At least I'll feel something.

Taliban, I don't even know what that means. All I know is that I should want this, I should want it.

BILKO *enters the bombed-out house.* GOLDIE *is gone. We still hear random gunfire.*

I should want this.

BILKO. Yeah? What is it?

CARL. Chocolate pudding in chocolate sauce.

BILKO. Right. You don't want it though, do you?

CARL. No.

BILKO. No. What you want to do is to get your arse up off the floor and get out there, we're moving forward.

CARL. Which way is that?

BILKO. Forward? It's forward dickhead. Out there, across the field.

CARL. Taliban across the field.

BILKO. Exactly. We're going to kill them, now come on. Are you alright?

CARL. Fucking starving.

BILKO. Yeah? Well I've heard that they've got a McDonald's in the next village so try and hold out until then eh?

CARL. Piss off.

BILKO. Are you coming or not?

CARL. Of course I am. British Army aren't I? Fuckin' best.

BILKO. And what do we do?

CARL. We fight, we win, we carry on.

BILKO. Good girl. Love you.

CARL. Yeah right, you too.

It takes a massive amount of effort but he stands and starts to walk. BILKO *stays still. Gunfire. The gunfire gets heavier and heavier during the following speech.*

We fight, we win, we carry on. Carry on and on and don't turn round. Never that.

His walk becomes a jog. He is beginning to shake off the fatigue. BILKO *stays still.*

Forward and onwards and burn this land. Burn this land and go home. Nah not that. Burn this land and carry on. Burn more lands and never look back, never go home. Bad here but worse there. Just keep going. Just dig deep and carry on. Thunder in my blood. Come on Bilko. March on. Here it comes Bilko. Here it comes. HERE IT COMES!

The gunfire intensifies.

MARCH ON BILKO!

CARL *begins to run. He is running hard. The gunfire intensifies further. As he runs* CARL *tries to compete with the gunfire, he shouts.*

WE FIGHT, WE WIN, WE BURN YOUR LAND.

He howls. He is running harder than ever. There is a massive amount of gunfire. Too much. BILKO *is stood still as* CARL *runs hard.* BILKO *is bleeding.*

WE FIGHT, WE WIN, WE DON'T TURN ROUND.

Heavy weapons fire. BILKO *bleeds heavily.*

MARCH ON BILKO. MARCH ON!!!

BILKO *falls.* CARL *tries to lift him and move him to safety. The noise stops.* CARL *stops, he's got* BILKO's *blood on his uniform and face.*

It's nothing, it's nothing, you're alright. Air support are on their way. Taliban have gone. It's fine, it's all good, it's nothing at all.

BILKO *is screaming in pain.*

Strong as they come Bilko. It's cool, we're safe here, we just need to wait. We just need to wait.

BILKO. Is it bad?

CARL. What? No. It's nothing man, you'll be fine.

BILKO. Shut up.

CARL. It's nothing.

BILKO. Are you scared? You sound scared Squirt.

CARL. No. We're scared of nothing Bilko. British Army, strong as they come.

BILKO. I'm scared.

CARL. You're not.

BILKO. I am. I'm scared. There isn't one person in this whole big country that isn't scared. Both sides, Squirt. From border to border it's nothing but fear. Is it bad?

CARL. No.

BILKO. Such a prick. Is it bad?

CARL. No Bilko it's gonna be alright.

BILKO. It's on me isn't it?

CARL. What?

BILKO. The Mark of Cain. It's on me.

CARL. What?

BILKO. It's on me Carl. It's on all of us.

CARL. Shut up man. It's just words.

BILKO. It's on me.

CARL. We did what we had to do. They're just words. It was us or them.

BILKO. Not all the time it wasn't.

CARL. It was man, shut up.

BILKO. He had his hands up. It's the Mark of Cain I know it is.

CARL. Shut the fuck up man. You're freaking me out.

BILKO. Good.

CARL. It's alright. It's a war isn't it?

BILKO. No. It's not war. This is an invasion. Fucking cold and clinical and he had his hands up.

CARL. Shut up Bilko man.

BILKO *is crying*.

BILKO. He had his hands up, he had his fucking hands up. It's on me, I know it is and I can't get it off... I'm really fuckin' scared Carl... I'm scared about what happens next.

BILKO *dies*.

CARL. Bilko? Bilko? You'll be alright mate. You'll be alright. Bilko. Wake up man. Fuckin' wake up Bilko.

CARL *is consumed by rage. He breaks away from* BILKO'*s body barely able to contain it*.

Taliban. Fuckin' Taliban, I'm gonna ruin them all, I'm gonna find them and ruin them all, every last one of them, hands up or hands down, I don't care. Put your hands up to me and I'll shoot you bandy. Good and dead. I'll fly my flag. I'll fly my flag in your bastard, dust-bowl, barren land for the rest of my born days. Watch me. Mark of Cain. Mark of Cain. Mark of Cain, I'll mark you Afghan man. I'll mark you with your own blood, your blood and my fury. This time it's gonna hurt you all! All of you! No time to rest, no time for sorrow, back to work and fight hard.

As the BILKO *scene dissolves behind him, a new scene at a standard weapons search emerges in the space. Soldiers are searching civilians. One* AFGHAN MAN *stands apart from the others.*

There's a man. Standard weapons search. Nothing special but there's a man standing in front of me, he's standing, he should be kneeling down like the rest of them. Should be kneeling. It's a standard weapons search, not allowed Abdul mate.

'Get on your knees. Get on your knees.'

It's hot today. Hot and there's thunder in my blood. It's properly, properly hot. It's hot like it's not been for ages, not since, not since... yeah, so what? Not since he died, not since he went and died. Dead like a loser. You lost Bilko. I won and I carry on. I fight, I win, I carry on.

Tight here, no room to run. Hot. Really hot today. He'd have blagged out of the search and got stripped down and soaked it up. He loved a tan, Bilko did. But he's dead and gone and I'm still standing boy. ME. Still standing. Still standing up. Standard weapons search and he's still standing up. I've seen this bloke before, I recognise him, he knows the drill. Why's he looking at me like that? Just standing up, all brave and smiling like he knows something, like he's better than me, like Goldie Shaw better than me in the rain. Too hot for this. Too tight for this.

'Get on your knees mate. Get on your knees mate. Stop looking at me and get on your knees mate. Stop smiling. Stop smiling. Stop laughing at me. Get on your knees. Stop smiling. I will do this. I will do this.'

He can't conjure anyone to stop him.

Choose a face. You. I'm out. GO. BANG.

CARL *head-butts the* AFGHAN MAN.

YES!

I've slotted him clean on the bridge and he's down. OVER.
He's on his knees now. I just popped it. I think it's broken
actually. He's making some noise now, maybe it did break it.
I broke his nose.

Bilko? Bilko man, I've done his nose. He's shouting. I can't
understand him. Bilko, I don't know what he's saying mate.
What should I do? Bilko? What should I do Bilko? What do
I do now? Now that you're not here. Bilko?

He kneels down. To the AFGHAN MAN.

Stop shouting mate. It's okay. I'll fix it. I promise. I'll fix it.
STOP SHOUTING OR I'LL DO IT AGAIN!!!!!! I'll fix it
for you, it's only your nose. I'll fix it, I promise.

The AFGHAN MAN *scene dissolves.* CARL *stands and
starts running hard and fast. It's strong and powerful and
chaotic. His speech is punctuated by his running. His
movement and words feed each other.*

If I don't fight then what do I do? What's it all been for after
all. After death, after people die, after thunder in my blood
and rage what has it been for? I don't want to fight any more.
We fight, we win, we carry on. I want to stop. Can't stop,
never stop it doesn't end until it's forced to stop. We fight,
we win, we fight some more. It doesn't stop.

All I can hear is my own voice. It doesn't stop until it's
forced to stop. We fight, we win, we carry, carry me on your
back when I'm dead Squirt? I did that. I did that Bilko and
now it's on my back on my shoulders. I carry everything
there, it doesn't go away, like a mark, like a stain, it's in my
bones like the rock. On me and in me and I've got to run it
off. Got to run. Got to run in the rain and wash it off. Get
back and run, get back, get back to being me.

All I can hear is my voice. My voice and guns and thunder in
my blood and I just want it to stop. Make it stop! Fucking
thunder. MAKE IT STOP! MAKE. IT. STOP.

CARL*'s* MUM *enters. She is not a ghost. She is a*
conversation in his head. He stops running but remains
mobile and active and energised until forced to stop.

MUM. Hello Carl love.

CARL. Alright Mum?

MUM. Everything okay?

CARL. What with me? Everything's absolutely seventy-five
hundred per cent crystal mustard with me Mum. How are you?

MUM. I'm fine. Are you going to sit down?

CARL. No.

MUM. Sit down Carl. Sit down with me. We haven't had a
good chat in ages have we?

CARL. Don't need to sit, don't need it, don't need anything any
more. I'm just me. All me, that's what I am. Me and free.

MUM. We're just talking love.

CARL. He's dead Mum. They killed him. They threw a grenade
and shot bullets, lots of bullets. He didn't die straight away
but they killed him Mum.

MUM. I know Carl.

CARL. I dragged him out. I dragged him out and carried him,
you know? They were firing at us but I carried him to the
trees until the air support came. He died. We ran out of time.
There was a lot of blood on me. Some of it went in my
mouth Mum.

MUM. I know.

CARL. He just died Mum. He just died. I saw his breath stop.

MUM. I know.

CARL. They're going to give me a medal. They made me a
Lance Corporal and they're going to give me a medal and I
don't want it. I don't want it. I don't care about it. I don't
care about anything. They've made me numb y'know? So
that I do things. That's what they do.

Is he with you now Mum?

MUM. We're just talking Carl. We're just talking.

CARL. I know.

MUM. Sit down Carl.

CARL. No time to stop, no time for sorrow.

MUM. Do you remember me?

CARL. What? I think so. Most days I think about you and Dad. We had fun didn't we? We had fun.

He laughs but it's out of pain. He is hurting hard now.

I remember some things.

MUM. I used to watch you.

CARL. Yeah?

MUM. Yeah. I used to watch you lots.

CARL. Still watching me now aren't you Mum?

MUM. Not any more Carl. No.

CARL. Right.

MUM. This isn't you Carl.

CARL. Too right it is. Free and me.

MUM. It's not my boy.

CARL. You died though Mum. You died and everything got messed up. We were rubbish without you. We broke.

I'm sorry Mum.

MUM. What for?

CARL. This.

I think I grew up wrong.

MUM. I used to watch you when you weren't looking, when you were just being you, just you. I'd stand there when it was just your body and your imagination together and you used to scare me. Not scare me but you amazed me, your potential amazed me Carl. You are pure. You are the purest thing I've ever known. You are totally pure and you don't even know what I mean do you?

CARL. No.

There are no words. She holds him. She makes him stop. He breaks. Heavy deep tears.

I'm sorry Mum. I'm sorry. I tried really hard.

MUM. There has to be time for sorrow. There has to be time for sorrow my boy. My little boy. My little boy. Sshhhh.

She holds him like a mother holds a child. When he finally stops, MUM *stands alone and sings 'As I Did Go' by Merry Hell. It's a memory of his childhood, it's a protest, it's a song at a funeral.*

The song ends and somewhere else in the space.
LIEUTENANT THOMPSON *appears. It is some time later.*
CARL *joins him.*

LIEUTENANT THOMPSON. Good to see you Jackson. How are you feeling?

CARL. Good sir, great sir, all A-okay with me sir.

LIEUTENANT THOMPSON. Do you feel that you are ready to go back to your unit Jackson?

CARL. Yes sir.

LIEUTENANT THOMPSON. And are you staying back?

CARL. I never went away sir.

LIEUTENANT THOMPSON. A simple 'yes sir' would suffice thank you.

CARL. Yes sir. Sorry sir. I'm like Take That sir.

LIEUTENANT THOMPSON. What?

CARL. Back for good sir.

LIEUTENANT THOMPSON. Good. Good. You've seen some action recently and you've been allowed some time on the base to recuperate. That is a privilege afforded someone who has been under a large amount of pressure. Would you say that you've been under a large amount of pressure Jackson?

CARL. Some sir, yes sir.

LIEUTENANT THOMPSON. How was it?

CARL. It was okay sir.

LIEUTENANT THOMPSON. Hard?

CARL. It was different each day sir. Some days were hard, some were easy. Have you been out there sir?

LIEUTENANT THOMPSON. I beg your pardon Jackson?

CARL. Afghanistan sir. Beautiful country sir. Have you been off base sir?

LIEUTENANT THOMPSON. This is my third tour Jackson and beautiful or not I am asking you these questions to enable me to fill out this form. The answers you give I will write down on this form here – this pretty pink form. I will then send it to someone who doesn't know or give a toss about you and they will process it. It will be typed up and processed and never seen again and you will go back to being a soldier. Now is that what you want?

CARL. Yes sir.

LIEUTENANT THOMPSON. So just answer the questions. Are you are ready, willing and able to see more action similar to or more intensive than what you have previously seen?

   CARL *doesn't respond.*

   Are you ready, willing and able to see more action Lance Corporal? More of the same or worse than previously seen?

CARL. Ready and able sir.

   Pause.

LIEUTENANT THOMPSON. And willing, Lance Corporal?

CARL. Ready and able sir.

LIEUTENANT THOMPSON. And willing Lance Corporal?

CARL. I'll fight for you sir. I'll fight hard, I always do.

LIEUTENANT THOMPSON. That isn't what I asked. Do I need to remind you where you are Lance Corporal? This is Afghanistan, this is a terrific war zone where people are in combat situations every minute of every single hour of every single day. This is a dangerous place to be, people will be relying on your concentration, on your commitment to the British Army and if you are not ready, WILLING and able to take yourself through what is required of you then you will be back home to whatever shithole part of England you came from with nothing but embarrassment for company. Is this sinking in Jackson? You've had a tough trot but you should be through that by now. You've had plenty of time –

CARL. Blackpool.

LIEUTENANT THOMPSON. What was that?

CARL. I'm from Blackpool sir.

LIEUTENANT THOMPSON. I don't care if you're from the Moon my lad, this is not the behaviour I expect or want to see from an emerging talent in the British Army. Control yourself and –

CARL. You said I'd see the world sir.

LIEUTENANT THOMPSON. Control yourself.

CARL. You said I'd see the world sir.

LIEUTENANT THOMPSON. I said no such thing to you, now stand down from here and –

CARL. YOU SAID I'D SEE THE WORLD SIR!

LIEUTENANT THOMPSON. STAND DOWN!

CARL. Do you know why I joined the Army sir?

LIEUTENANT THOMPSON. I don't give a damn.

CARL. NO!

LIEUTENANT THOMPSON. This is over.

> LIEUTENANT THOMPSON *goes to leave but is held back by what* CARL *says next.*

CARL. I joined the Army because I couldn't get a job on civvy
street, couldn't get one, didn't want one. I didn't want to get
stuck in a down, brown, empty old town, I didn't want to be
working for the weekend and wasting the week. I wanted
more. More for me please sir, more. So I signed up. You said
I'd do well, you said I'd see the world. Who were you
talking to sir? You didn't have a fuckin' clue did you? Just a
face, a nameless no one, with fire in his eyes and two strong
legs. I bit your bastard hand off didn't I sir? Because I'd 'do
well,' I'd 'see the world.' All you needed to do then was
chuck in a bit of national pride and I'd be the perfect
clockwork soldier. Rule Britannia, Cruel Britannia, show me
how to fool Britannia. I've seen it all sir, Kenya, Germany,
Afghanistan sir. Yes sir! It's true sir. You did show me the
world sir. I saw a gay bloke get kicked to death in Hamburg.
I saw two black lads get pissed on every day for a month in
Nairobi. I saw a soldier walk away from a dying child and
I've seen grenades and bullets blow the arse out of men,
more than men. Join up, keep up, put and shut up! No more
sir! It's not tanks and ranks and firing blanks! It's live rounds
and paid in pounds. Sterling. Rule Britannia? It's bullshit.
Britannia waives the rules and I think you know it sir.

LIEUTENANT THOMPSON. Are you finished? ARE YOU
FINISHED JACKSON?

CARL. NO! MY BUSINESS NOW IS NORTH!! It's alright.
My business now is north.

Somewhere in the space the British Legion forms. CARL
*goes to the bar, downs a whiskey and takes a pint. He places
the whistle on the table and sits exactly as* UNCLE
CHARLES *was described – leaning over the back of a bench
chair, looking out of a window at nothing. He bites his nails.
There is silence. All we can hear is the sound of his teeth
hitting together as they crack through his fingernails.* ANDY
*enters. He looks different, cleaner, clearer than before. He
goes to the bar, turns and sees* CARL.

ANDY. Carl.

He doesn't respond.

Carl. Alright Carl it's Andy. Andy Appleton – How you
doing our kid? Fuckin' wicked. Back from the front line and
all that? Good to see you man.

CARL. Alright?

ANDY. Yeah. Yeah sound y'know. What're you doing here?
Fuckin' AWOL for some candyfloss or summat?

CARL. No. I'm out. Jacked it, sacked it, packed it in mate.

ANDY. Fuck off. What for?

CARL. It got old y'know?

ANDY. Right. Shit. That's bad man. You're a proper hero round
here our kid. Get yourself in a uniform and pack off to
Afghanistan and they love you. That and the football team,
like. Everyone's had claims on you round here Carl. Goldie
was like the Oracle or whatever. How's Carl? Is he still
alive? Where is he now? All that shit. She had all the
answers. Proper overnight-hero stuff mate. She's havin' a kid
now Goldie. Proper settled and shit, I think she's moved out
of Blackpool. Down south somewhere. Don't blame her, it's
shit round here. Hey, don't go telling the birds that you've
jacked in the Army Carl. Use it our kid, use that shit.

CARL. Where's your Anthony?

ANDY. Inside. Three and a half years – possession with the
intent to supply or summat.

CARL. How's he doing?

ANDY. Yeah he loves it ta. They get KFC twice a week and
he's selling more in there than he ever did.

CARL. You got anything on you?

ANDY. No I'm off it mate.

CARL. Can you get some?

ANDY. No chance our kid. They put me on a programme.
Clean as a whistle for nine months now, they give you a job
an' all. You won't believe it mate. School caretaker at St
Catherine's, that posh one near Fleetwood. The posh mums

proper love me – All I do is sit in a shed at the bottom of the playing field. I just sit there surrounded by bog roll and listen to the cricket most days. It's top.

CARL *has stopped listening.*

Did you kill anyone?

CARL. What? No.

ANDY. No? Right. All that time and you didn't slot anyone? That's a bit boring. You can't think about it can you? You can't let it hassle with your head after you've nailed someone. I'd be sound with that, nothing bothers me. Especially if it's allowed like.

CARL. Do it then.

ANDY. How d'ya mean?

CARL. Do it.

ANDY. Do what?

CARL. Go. Do it. Join up. Do it. Make yourself a hero Andy.

ANDY. Fuck that.

CARL. Do it. Why not?

ANDY. All that exercise. I'd be all over the place our kid. I've got asthma.

CARL. Do it.

ANDY. Nah I'm alright cheers.

CARL. FUCKING DO IT. For me. For Blackpool's newest top-class hero soldier boy. Do it. Get in Andy. Get in and be proper excited. Get in and be all excited and get led by the knob into stuff you can't get out of Andy.

ANDY. Alright, calm down Carl.

CARL. Do it. Do the big stuff Andy. It's not like selling scag, you don't get put in a cell with a Bargain Bucket mate. They let you go, they let you walk away and they let you fucking deal with it. It's cool. Do it. Do it cunt. Do it cunt. Do it.

ANDY. Alright Carl. You're pissed man.

CARL advances towards him all clumsily.

Get away from me Carl.

CARL. What you gonna do, cry? Don't bother, it doesn't work, I'll kill you anyway. You can cry until the colour falls out of your eyes, until they're all white and there's no colour left. You can beg in whatever language you want to and I'll still drop you. I'll kill you whatever you are.

CARL grabs hold of ANDY and sits him down. He keeps hold of him throughout the next section. He looks him in the eye throughout.

ANDY. Get off me Carl. Get off, leave me alone.

CARL. I've seen your death boy. I've seen you dead in front of me. I've seen you with your head open and a starving dog eating your brain. Your brain was keeping a mangy old starving dog alive. Survival of the shittest. I saw it. Out there – that's how I did it, that's how I managed it in my head you know? When I did that, when I did what I did, when I shot people that I didn't know, I made it like I did know them. I gave them faces that I did know to make it better. You, you were one, you were the one with the dog. I put your face on him and I fired. Anthony, my old man, my Uncle Charles, Goldie Shaw she got it loads, her dad, her mum, Mr Buckley from school. Anyone. Not anyone. No. Not anyone. People. Your Alison. I shot her head clean off more than anyone else, more times than I can remember mate – your sister – bosh, dead. Brains all over the place. Lumps. It made it better. Because they could have been anyone out there, I could have been aiming at anyone, they could have been good, you know, fucking brilliant – they could have found the cure for cancer or something! So I shot at you lot instead and it made it better. At least with you lot I knew you were half-dead anyway. Waste. Cancer. They could have found the cure for cancer.

CARL releases ANDY.

ANDY. You're twisted mate. D'ya hear me Carl? You're fuckin' loopy man.

But CARL*'s mind is elsewhere now, he is volatile and tense but distant, weighed down – there is no outlet any more. He turns and looks out of the steamed-up window.* ANDY *exits.* CARL *looks out of the steamed-up window and talks to no one.*

CARL. It's in your bones like the fucking rock. It's in you, it's in you all and you'll never get it out.

He is still for the first time. After some time he picks up the whistle, looks at it, he takes a breath, puts the whistle in his mouth, holds it there, takes it out again without blowing it. He puts it back on the table and looks at it. His energy has gone. After some time he takes a long drink of his pint and stands. He stands to attention, pint in hand, and recites a poem.

My meteoric rise you called it,
My meteoric rise to success,
An elevation through ranks for excellence and skill,
An addiction to being the best.

You gave me a mission and I managed to complete it,
You gave me an order and I obeyed,
Your puzzles I solved, your miles I ran,
Your country's pride I conveyed.

For years I listened and acted your orders,
For years I battled with thought,
Because to think would be to ruin your little regime,
Of winning your battles I fought.

My sweat, my blood, my hard-gritted teeth,
My fear, my shame of my actions.
My tenacity, my audacity, my outright absurdity,
My ignoring the feelings beneath.

But here I am in my backstreet barracks,
And I ask, 'What did I expect after all?'
Because a meteoric rise is a perfect description,
Because meteors don't rise, they fall.

METEORS DON'T RISE THEY FALL!!!

Blackout.

Situated in the heart of Manchester, the Royal Exchange is one of the UK's leading producing theatres. The company nurtures outstanding creative talent in Manchester and attracts some of the most original artists and theatre-makers in the country to present high-quality classic plays and new writing to entertain, provoke and inspire.

The company is committed to supporting and developing new writing. In partnership with property company, Bruntwood, it runs the bi-annual Bruntwood Prize for Playwriting – the UK's biggest playwriting competition. *Britannia Waves the Rules* was a 2011 Bruntwood Prize for Playwriting winner.

In the last year the Royal Exchange has presented six world premieres – Bruntwood Prize-winning plays *Brilliant Adventures* by Alistair McDowall and *Three Birds* by Janice Okoh, as well as Rory Mullarkey's *Cannibals*, Mike Kenny's *Edmund the Learned Pig*, *There Has Possibly Been an Incident* by Chris Thorpe and *Britannia Waves the Rules* which runs from 26 May to 7 June 2014.

Royal Exchange Theatre, St. Ann's Square, Manchester, M2 7DH
www.royalexchange.co.uk, +44 161 833 9333
Registered Charity Number 255424

www.nickhernbooks.co.uk

facebook.com/nickhernbooks

twitter.com/nickhernbooks